BASIC.WE ARE CHURCH

FOLLOWER'S GUIDE

BASIC.WE ARE CHURCH

FOLLOWER'S GUIDE

FRANCIS CHAN
with Mark Beuving

David C Cook®
transforming lives together

BASIC.WE ARE CHURCH FOLLOWER'S GUIDE
Published by David C Cook
4050 Lee Vance View
Colorado Springs, CO 80918 U.S.A.

David C Cook Distribution Canada
55 Woodslee Avenue, Paris, Ontario, Canada N3L 3E5

David C Cook U.K., Kingsway Communications
Eastbourne, East Sussex BN23 6NT, England

The graphic circle C logo is a registered trademark of David C Cook.

All rights reserved. Except for brief excerpts for review purposes,
no part of this book may be reproduced or used in any form
without written permission from the publisher.

All Scripture quotations are taken from *The Holy Bible, English Standard
Version.* Copyright © 2000; 2001 by Crossway Bibles, a division of Good
News Publishers. Used by permission. All rights reserved.
The author has added italics to Scripture quotations for emphasis.

ISBN 978-0-7814-0385-6
eISBN 978-0-7814-0792-2

© 2011 David C Cook

Printed in the United States of America
First Edition 2011

4 5 6 7 8 9 10 11

071415

Contents

Introduction

Welcome to the *BASIC. WE ARE CHURCH Follower's Guide*. This workbook is designed to help you think through the material that you will be watching in the *WE ARE CHURCH* films and discussing as a group. I'm sure that you'll be challenged as you watch the four films (*FELLOWSHIP, TEACHING, PRAYER,* and *COMMUNION*). And I'm confident that your small group discussions will help you process the material in those films. But if you stop with those two things, I think you'll be missing out.

That's why we've included this *Follower's Guide*. As challenging as the films are, I'm afraid that once the reality of everyday life sets in, the conviction you feel will be drowned out by a tidal wave of distractions. This workbook offers you the opportunity to take what you've seen in the films and what you've discussed with your small group and sit with it. My prayer is that you will approach each of the nine sessions in this workbook patiently and prayerfully.

A *Follower's Guide* like this isn't effective unless you're prepared to examine your heart and open up your life to the truth of God's Word. You could read through each of the sessions in just a few minutes, but I hope you won't move that quickly. I've built in times for prayer, thoughtful meditation, and Bible study. The more you allow the material to soak in, the more you'll get out of this process. I challenge you to meditate on the Scripture presented, honestly examine your heart, and push yourself to apply what you're studying to your everyday life.

The material in these sessions will lead you to think about what we do as a church and why we do those basic things. We all have ideas about what the church should be and do, but those ideas are often formed more by our own experiences with the church than by what God says in the Bible about the church. My prayer is that you will see these four basic practices freshly and that your life will be changed as a result.

The BASIC Process

For each of the four films included in the *BASIC.WE ARE CHURCH A Small Group Experience* box set, we've created two *Follower's Guide* sessions for individual study, along with a ninth session at the end to help you put into practice what you've explored. So once you've discussed each *BASIC.WE ARE CHURCH* session with your small group, use this *Follower's Guide* on your own to go deeper into that topic. The sessions in this *Follower's Guide* are designed to be worked through *after* you've watched the corresponding BASIC film and discussed the corresponding small-group session, which are on the *BASIC.WE ARE CHURCH* DVDs.

So the process for getting the most out of the BASIC films goes like this:

1. You view the film *FELLOWSHIP* with your small group.

2. On the *FELLOWSHIP* disc, return to the top menu and select "Session 1." Question 1 will appear on your screen. Discuss

that question, then click [Next] for question 2, and so on until
the end of the discussion.

3. Make sure each person in the group has a copy of this *Follower's
   Guide*. After your discussion of Session 1 on the DVD, go
   home and take about an hour on your own to think and pray
   through the questions for *FELLOWSHIP* Session 1 in this
   guide. Write notes in the space provided. This is your chance to
   decide if you are truly on board with what God is saying to you
   in *FELLOWSHIP*.

4. Gather with your group for your next discussion. On the
   FELLOWSHIP DVD menu screen, select "Session 2." Discuss
   each question in turn. Session 2 includes clips from the film, so
   you don't have to view the entire film again if you choose not
   to. If you prefer, though, you can always view the whole film
   again.

5. Think and pray through *FELLOWSHIP* Session 2 in this
   Follower's Guide on your own.

6. Repeat this same process for *TEACHING, PRAYER,* and
   COMMUNION. The *COMMUNION* disc also includes a
   ninth discussion session called "BASIC.LIVING."

7. Lastly, think and pray through the BASIC.LIVING session in
   this *Follower's Guide*.

If you're leading a discussion group through *BASIC. WE ARE CHURCH*, check out the Tips for Leaders at the end of this guide. (The Extras DVD also has a downloadable PDF of the Tips for Leaders section.)

FELLOWSHIP
Session 1

When I was in school, I always hated group projects. I'm the type of person who would much rather do a school project on my own than work together with other people. For one thing, it's terribly inconvenient. You have to find a place to meet, coordinate schedules, and together decide how you're going to tackle the project. And then there's the reality that group work is often inefficient. When I'm working alone, I can seclude myself and work at my own pace until the project is done. In group work, on the other hand, there are always distractions, and I can't choose the pace because not everyone works the same way. And we all know those people who don't do their share of the work. Group work can be unbelievably frustrating.

I have sometimes portrayed this desire to work alone in positive terms. I would describe myself as a perfectionist or explain that I just really want to be productive. Sometimes I would even claim that I didn't want to put the work on other people—as if my individualism was focused on serving others.

But when it really comes down to it, my desire to work alone is all about self-reliance. Relying on other people can be messy, and the job doesn't always get done according to my expectations. When I rely on myself, I set the terms and determine the outcome—or so I think.

This type of individualism is almost universal among Westerners. We're raised with the mind-set that we create our own identities and shape our own destinies. We're taught to pull ourselves up by our bootstraps. If you believe it, you can achieve it—even if the whole world tries to stand in your way.

I'm always amazed at how naturally the values and assumptions of our culture creep into our Christianity. Growing up, I was told that the most important thing was my personal relationship with Jesus Christ. He is my personal Lord and Savior. My devotional life always consisted of getting away from everyone else and focusing on "me and God."

Now, I want to be quick to say that these things aren't bad. My personal relationship with Jesus is vitally important, He is my personal Savior, and I still believe that it's important to spend time alone with God. But for most of my Christian life, the emphasis was on me as an individual. I rarely considered the fact that I was a part of something bigger than myself, that I was a part of the people of God, or that my faith ought to be tied to the faith of the Christians around me. Basically, my spiritual life was very individualistic, very self-reliant. Ironically, I know that I'm not alone in my individualism.

1. Take a minute to analyze your life. Do you tend to be individualistic and self-reliant? If so, how does that individualism manifest itself in your life? If not, how do you see individualism affecting the church?

2. Think about the way you view the other Christians in your life. Do you see them merely as separate individuals, or do see yourself as inseparably connected to them?

My life changed drastically when I finally realized that I *need* other Christians in my life. As important as my own personal relationship with Jesus is, I cannot live out my God-given mission of making disciples without other Christians. Once my mind-set shifted in this regard, I began to notice how many times the Bible emphasizes the importance of working together with other Christians, of serving one another, of relying on one another. The Bible addresses this in many places, but I'd like to spend the rest of this session thinking through Ephesians 2.

I've never met a Christian who doesn't love Ephesians 2:1–10. Paul started off by looking back at our spiritual state before Christ and declaring that we were just like every other person in the world—unresponsive to God's glory, absorbed in our passions and desires, and utterly without hope. This isn't a comfortable truth to think through, but it makes Paul's next statements incredibly potent:

But God, being rich in mercy, because of the great love with which he loved us, even when we were dead in our trespasses, made us alive together with Christ—by grace you have been saved. (Ephesians 2:4–5)

With these words, the miracle of the gospel hits us square in the face. We all resonate with the truth of Ephesians 2:1–10.

But I have found that most Christians are less familiar with Ephesians 2:11–22. In this passage, Paul presented the same concepts and applied them not to our individual salvation experiences but to our inclusion in the people of God. He used the same stark imagery to describe the separation that we all experienced and to highlight the interpersonal reconciliation that comes through the gospel.

3. Stop for a minute and read carefully through Ephesians 2:11–22. When you've read and thought about it for a while, write down what stands out to you. What are the passage's themes? How do they relate to the themes in Ephesians 2:1–10?

Verses 1–10 seem to focus on us as individuals, but verses 11–22 highlight some corporate aspects of our salvation.

In verses 11–18 Paul wrote about how Jesus' death reconciled two groups who had nothing but contempt for each other: the Jews (who were God's chosen people and viewed Gentiles as filth) and the Gentiles (non-Jews who knew nothing of God's promises and who thought Jewish beliefs and practices were bizarre). The Gentiles were hopeless when it came to salvation, just as individually (verses 1–3) we were dead and hopeless. But parallel to verses 4–5, this bleak situation only highlights the miracle of Christ:

> *But now in Christ Jesus* you who once were far off have been brought near by the blood of Christ. For he himself is our peace, who has made us both one and has broken down in his flesh the dividing wall of hostility by abolishing the law of commandments expressed in ordinances, that he might create in himself one new man in place of the two, so making peace, and might reconcile us both to God in one body through the cross, thereby killing the hostility. (Ephesians 2:13–16)

Two groups of people were completely at odds with each other, and Jesus died to make those two groups into one. Jesus tore down the dividing wall of hostility, He created one new man in place of the two, He reconciled us to God in one body, and He killed the enmity.

4. Do you have any negative thoughts about other Christians, either individuals or groups? If so, what are some of those negative thoughts? (For example, "Person X isn't really serious about his faith" or "Group Y has bad doctrine" or "So-and-so is annoying and has nothing valuable to contribute.") Be as specific as you can.

If Jesus wants us to be united with other Christians so badly that He sacrificed Himself in order to make it happen, then who are we to say—whether actively with our words or passively with our lifestyles—that working together with other Christians doesn't really matter?

Paul wasn't simply describing an event where Jews and Gentiles forgive one another and then go their own separate ways. No, he was describing a new creation of God. Just as he described a Christian being re-created from something dead into something alive (verse 5), he described Jesus taking two alienated groups and re-creating them into a single group that now functions as one entity:

> So then you are no longer strangers and aliens, but you are fellow citizens with the saints and members of the household of God, built on the foundation of the apostles and prophets, Christ Jesus himself being the cornerstone, in whom the whole structure, being joined together, grows into a holy temple in the Lord. In him you also are being built together into a dwelling place for God by the Spirit. (Ephesians 2:19–22)

5. Consider the words and phrases Paul used in this passage to describe Christians. Which of the following can you be or do on your own, and which do you have to be or do with others? In each case, why?

Fellow citizens with the saints

Members of the household of God

The whole structure, being joined together, grows into a holy temple in the Lord

Built together into a dwelling place for God

6. Someone might say, "Okay, we're all one *spiritual* household, one dwelling place for God *spiritually*, but that doesn't mean we need to be

together *physically* when we serve or worship God." How would you respond?

7. If Jesus died to join you together with other believers so that you can all collectively serve as the temple of the Holy Spirit, how should that affect the way you look at the Christians around you?

The church is not a building made of wood or stones, but a house made up of individual people who are miraculously joined together by the death of Christ to be the place where God dwells on earth. Together we become a dwelling place for the Spirit of God. Yes, each of our bodies is a temple of the Holy Spirit. But here Paul said that all of God's people collectively are one big temple in which the Spirit of God dwells. It's not about me as an individual; it's about the group of people whom God has re-created to be something bigger than any one individual.

8. Try to take some practical steps here. If being joined together with the Christians around you is absolutely essential to the Christian life, what steps can you begin taking immediately that will help make this ideal into a reality?

Depending on where you are in the process of seeing the need for fellowship and true unity with other Christians, you could be at the start of an incredible journey. I still have to fight my tendency toward individualism (group work is still difficult at times), but I am constantly reminded of the benefits of sharing life with other Christians. Even if you've been thinking along these lines for some time, you still have a lot of work ahead of you. But either way, it starts with a shift in your mentality. You will not experience true fellowship until you begin to love the people around you and understand at a fundamental level that you need them in your life. You may not have chosen the other Christians in your life; I often find myself working together with people who are unbelievably different from me. But there is great comfort in knowing that God chose them and placed them in your life.

9. Before you move on with your day, spend some time praying. Ask God to change your mind-set, to renew your mind. Ask Him to continue hitting you with the importance of living in fellowship with the Christians around

you. Ask Him to give you a genuine love for those people. And before you stop, spend some time praying for the needs and spiritual health of your fellow members in the household of God.

FELLOWSHIP
Session 2

Many Christians misunderstand the concept of fellowship because they misunderstand themselves. As much as we'd like to set our own agendas and focus on the things we find appealing, God has created each of us in a specific way for a specific reason. God has shaped us into the people we are, not so that we can fulfill our own purposes, but so that we can minister on His behalf to the people around us.

1. Read through 1 Corinthians 12. As you read, try to pay attention to what Paul wrote about (1) the spiritual gifts that God gives to each Christian, (2) God's purpose in giving those gifts, and (3) the result of Christians using these gifts appropriately.

Examples of gifts:

God's purpose in giving these gifts:

What results when groups of Christians use these gifts appropriately:

In this passage, Paul said that the Holy Spirit manifests Himself in the life of every Christian. These manifestations are referred to as "spiritual gifts"— supernatural abilities that are empowered by the Holy Spirit. Some of these gifts are overtly supernatural, like speaking in tongues or healing people. Others are subtler, but no less supernatural, such as encouragement, service, hospitality, and teaching. With these gifts, the Spirit empowers us to do these "ordinary" activities to a supernatural degree and with supernatural effectiveness. As an example, we're all called to encourage the people around us, but some Christians are divinely enabled to speak encouraging words to the right people at the right time, and God uses that encouragement to build up the church.

If you are a Christian, God has created you in a unique way and given you supernatural gifts to enable you to fulfill your God-given part in the church's mission of making disciples. You may need to figure out what your gifts are, but the Spirit has gifted you according to His will.

2. Think through the way that God has uniquely gifted you. Write down the things that God has enabled you to do well (such as encouraging other people, teaching, serving behind the scenes, praying for people, listening to people, or helping them through their problems).

This type of service to other people is the very reason that the Spirit empowers us in these ways. These aren't gifts that we can either use for ourselves or use for the benefit of others, depending on how we feel. No, the Spirit empowers us to do these things in supernatural ways *so that* we can effectively build up the Christians around us. Paul said this explicitly: "To each is given the manifestation of the Spirit *for the common good*" (1 Corinthians 12:7).

It means that if you find yourself using your gifts in a way that benefits you and no one else, you're misusing the gift of God! And that's a serious thing.

All of this ties in with the theme of fellowship. Our Christian life is not meant to be lived in isolation. God designed us to be Christians in the context of a community of believers who share their lives and serve one another, and the Holy Spirit manifests Himself in our lives in special ways so that we can do this to a supernatural degree!

3. To what extent do you tend to view your unique talents and gifts in terms of achieving your own goals? To what extent do you view them in terms of serving the people around you?

I can think of several individuals who seem supernaturally empowered to serve the people around them in a variety of ways. Every time I'm with them, I'm certain that they're doing exactly what God created them to do. And the beautiful thing is that they're not doing it for themselves, they're doing it for the sake of the people around them. The more these people serve, the closer our fellowship becomes.

4. Do you know Christians who have used their gifts to bless you? Write down a couple of examples.

5. When Christians begin to use God's blessings for the benefit of the people around them, the level of fellowship intensifies. Why is this type of fellowship so healthy?

6. What did Paul say in 1 Corinthians 12:21–26 about individualism and self-reliance?

As cool as an eye is, nobody wants to see a random eye trying to operate on its own apart from a body. We should think of a Christian trying to operate autonomously as equally disturbing. How can one Christian say explicitly or act as if they did not belong to the Christians around them? An individual Christian only makes sense in the context of a larger body: "The body does not consist of one member but of many" (1 Corinthians 12:14).

7. Can you think of a time when you downplayed the gifts of the Christians around you? What do you think motivated you to do this?

I find one of Paul's statements in this passage particularly intriguing. He said, "If one member suffers, all suffer together; if one member is honored, all rejoice together" (1 Corinthians 12:26). In terms of our physical bodies, this is a vivid illustration. We all know what it's like to have an injured toe or finger—the rest of your body knows exactly which part is in pain, and it immediately responds!

I have experienced this type of intimacy with other Christians. I have cried as people that I care deeply about shared their trials, and I have rejoiced alongside friends who were experiencing God's blessing in a tangible way. There is no shortcut to this type of close fellowship. It comes naturally as you work together for the sake of the gospel and invest in the lives of the Christians around you.

8. Have you ever experienced this type of close fellowship where every member of the group suffers or rejoices together? If so, describe what that was like. If not, what do you think has gotten in the way?

9. What can you do to help guide your group to this type of intimacy?

Paul's illustration of the church as a body only works if the Spirit is binding the individual believers together. "Now there are varieties of gifts, *but the same Spirit*; and there are varieties of service, *but the same Lord*; and there are varieties of activities, *but it is the same God* who empowers them all in everyone. To each is given the manifestation of the Spirit for the common good" (1 Corinthians 12:4–7).

This isn't something that can be forced. It comes through understanding that you have been blessed so that you can in turn bless the people around you. It comes through discovering the ways in which the Spirit is manifesting His power in your life and using those supernatural abilities to serve the Christians around you. And it comes through realizing that you are incomplete without the Spirit-empowered gifts of the other Christians in your life. Ultimately our churches will begin to look more and more like a well-functioning body as the Holy Spirit transforms our minds and empowers us to live "for the common good."

10. Look back to the gifts and abilities you listed in question 2. Copy them below, but this time add a second column for the needs of the people around you. Think through the needs that you are aware of, and list those

needs next to the gifting that would enable you to meet that need in some form.

Gifts   Needs

11. Spend some time praying about this list. What steps would you need to take in order to use the Spirit's unique manifestations in your life to meet the needs of the people listed above? Ask the Spirit to direct and empower you to build up the body of Christ.

Sometimes we get disappointed and start to give up if we don't see immediate results. I can tell you right now that at some point the Christians around you will let you down. But keep in mind that the response of the Christians around you is not the point of Paul's message in 1 Corinthians 12. He is trying to convince us to change the way we look at the church. It's not a place to get our needs met in a consumerist way. It's a living body, a thriving community. It's not about what I can get, it's about who I can serve. It's true that we need the other members of the body, but if our minds are set on serving the people around us, we will be too focused on the common good to be concerned about not having our needs met. And as the Spirit supernaturally empowers us to serve the other members of the body, we can trust Him to create the close fellowship that we long for.

TEACHING
Session 1

Luke said that the early church *devoted themselves* to the apostles' teaching (Acts 2:42). I find myself wondering what that must have looked like. I'm fairly diligent when it comes to studying the Bible, but can I really say that I have *devoted myself* to studying God's Word?

Luke's language also leads me back to Peter's call to long for the Word of God in the same way that a baby longs for its mother's milk (1 Peter 2:2). Can I really compare my attitude toward Scripture to an infant crying out for the one thing that sustains its life? These types of statements are so simple, but they carry such profound truths. If we took them seriously, they could radically change our lives.

1. Compare your own experience with the Bible to these two illustrations. Could you say that you have devoted yourself to the Bible or that you long for the Word of God like a newborn baby longs for milk? How

would you explain the discrepancy between these biblical illustrations
and your life?

It takes more than discipline to live up to this biblical calling. For one
thing, Peter's illustrations can't be appropriated simply by trying harder.
Longing for the Word of God may require you to change your schedule, but
it also involves a change of heart. I'm not advocating a lack of discipline, but
at some point we have to move beyond external behavior and address the
heart.

One of the best ways to develop a longing for the Word of God is to
first allow yourself to be struck by the nature of Scripture. If the Bible is just
another book that we're being pressured to read, then Bible study will seem
like a chore. But if we begin to view it as the very words of God—personal
communication from almighty God telling us of His love for us and His
mission for our lives—then we might actually begin to desire God's Word.

Start by considering this amazing statement about the nature of Scripture
by the author of Hebrews: "The word of God is living and active, sharper than
any two-edged sword, piercing to the division of soul and of spirit, of joints and
of marrow, and discerning the thoughts and intentions of the heart" (4:12).

The power of Scripture could hardly be stated more strongly. These reali-
ties immediately differentiate the Bible from every other book on our shelves
and every other activity we've been meaning to get around to.

2. Take a minute to think through this statement: *The Word of God is living and active.* What does it mean? What are the implications of this incredible statement?

3. Take a minute to think through this statement: *The Word of God discerns the thoughts and intentions of the heart.* What does it mean? What are the implications?

As you saw in the *TEACHING* film, we should all be teaching one another. But the only way to keep such a group from degenerating into an ongoing argument where every person passionately defends his or her own opinion is for each person to be grounded in Scripture. As we develop a passion for the Word of God, it will begin to transform us and the people around us.

4. Think through some of the benefits of growing stronger in your study of the Bible. Think of ways that this would benefit you personally and ways that it would benefit the other Christians around you. Make some notes below.

Benefits for you:

Benefits for the Christians around you:

As passionate as we may be for the Word of God, we will also encounter obstacles that will try to keep us from devoting ourselves to it. Unless you're willing to discover what these obstacles are and take practical steps toward removing them, you're going to be frustrated constantly when studying the Bible stays low on your priority list.

5. Think of some barriers that keep you from devoting yourself to the Bible. What is it that keeps you from diving into the Bible and craving the Word of God as an absolute necessity? As you think through these barriers, also take some time to think through how you can begin to overcome each obstacle. Make some notes below.

Barriers:

Plans for overcoming those barriers:

As we begin to throw ourselves into studying the Word of God, we should find our boldness increasing. In the Bible, God reveals Himself to us. We find God's perspective on who He is, who we are, and the way this world operates. The more we study Scripture, the more confident we become in the answers that God gives to life's most important questions. This confidence in the Word of God should lead us to teach the other people in our lives. As we find that the Bible answers the questions they're wrestling with and speaks to the troubles they're facing, we develop an appropriate boldness in the fact that we can share God's heart with the people in our lives.

But as with anything good, there are potential dangers. The problem is that we don't always differentiate between the eternal and unchanging nature of God's truth and our own incomplete and often inaccurate perception of what the Word of God is saying. I'm not at all trying to say that we can't know God's Word truly. Rather, I'm suggesting that we don't know God's truth comprehensively, which can lead us to an incomplete and therefore skewed understanding of God's truth.

So how do we balance the boldness that comes through knowledge of the Bible with our inability to see all of God's truth completely or perfectly? I believe the answer is humility. We can and should stand boldly on God's truth, but we must do so with a humility that allows for the possibility that we might be wrong. We should always be bold about what God says but humble about the way we understand what God says.

I believe that's what Paul had in mind when he told us not to "go beyond what is written," so that "none of you may be puffed up in favor of one against another" (1 Corinthians 4:6). As soon as we step beyond the simple statements of Scripture and stand firm on our interpretations of these scriptural statements, we are in danger of acting in pride.

Take some time to think through this balance. What does it look like to be bold in the Scriptures but humble in our interpretations?

6. Start with the boldness we should gain from the Scriptures. How should a confidence in the Word of God lead you to stand boldly on God's truth? How might that confidence manifest itself in concrete situations that you face?

7. Now consider the humility that we ought to have as individual human
beings who see only a part of the picture. How should your boldness
be tempered by a humility that recognizes that you don't have all the
answers? How might that humility manifest itself in concrete situations
that you face?

One important way of fostering this type of humility is to study the
Scriptures in fellowship with other Christians. As you learn and grow in your
understanding of the Bible, you can also learn from the ways in which the
other Christians in your life are learning and growing in their understanding
of the Bible. This is really what it means to be teaching one another. It's not
about you dogmatically sharing your views, whether those views are about the
Bible or politics. Instead, it's about everyone learning together from the Word
of God and then sharing what they've learned in humility and love.

8. If studying the Bible in close fellowship with other Christians is the ideal,
then what can you do to start making that happen with the Christians
around you? Even if they are resistant to the idea, how can you begin to
make this concept a reality in the life of your church body?

9. Before you walk away from this session, spend some time praying about the things you've been considering. These foundational truths often have simple answers, and that simplicity can lead us to think that they are easily adopted into our lifestyles. That's not typically the case. Spend some time asking God to increase your desire for His Word. Ask Him to guide you into a lifestyle that is devoted to knowing His Word and using that knowledge to love Him and the people around you to a greater extent. Pray that God would transform your group as you teach the Word of God to each other.

TEACHING
Session 2

I have always liked Paul's portrayal of the Christian life as a race in which he pressed on to reach the prize (Philippians 3:12–14). In the past, I tended to view myself as an individual runner in this race—I was racing against everyone else. My goal was to run the race well and reach the finish line. I had no concern for whether or not anyone else crossed the finish line.

But the Christian life is not that type of race. When we discussed the concept of fellowship, we said that God designed us to work together and rely on one another as the church. If we apply this idea to Paul's race imagery, then it isn't a me-against-the-world type of race. Instead, it's a three-legged race where one of your legs is strapped to the leg of the person next to you. And depending on how many Christians God has placed around you, this is a many-legged race. It's not about me crossing the finish line alone; it's about all of us crossing the finish line together.

The reality of the church is that I am not responsible only for my own spiritual growth; I am also responsible for the people God has placed in my life. It should matter to me that those people "attain the prize" as well. This comes to the forefront when we talk about the biblical concept of teaching.

Teaching is not about me building myself up—it's about me strengthening the people around me. Teaching is an inherently selfless act (or at least it should be). If all that mattered was my own spiritual growth, then I would just study the Bible on my own and never share with anyone else. But that's not the way God designed the church to function.

The church is designed to be a beautiful give-and-take where every person learns and grows and takes the time to help the people around him or her learn and grow at the same time. In this type of community, everyone is involved in the discipleship process and no one is off the hook.

1. Think about your involvement with the other Christians in your life. Has your interaction with them been focused on helping them to learn and grow? If so, how? If not, why not?

Teaching is an essential part of how we are meant to operate as the church. But how do you know what role you are called to play with regard to teaching? Paul framed our thinking on this issue in Ephesians 4. After explaining that God has given gifts to every Christian (a concept that we explored in talking about fellowship), Paul pointed out that God gave specific individuals—apostles, prophets, evangelists, pastors, and teachers—to the church for the purpose of training the rest of us to do the work of ministry.

Whereas most Christians think the pastor is the one who is supposed to be ministering, Paul said the pastor's job is to train the rest of us to minister to the people in our lives. How should this play out? Paul answered that question in verses 15–16:

> Speaking the truth in love, we are to grow up in every way into him who is the head, into Christ, from whom the whole body, joined and held together by every joint with which it is equipped, when each part is working properly, makes the body grow so that it builds itself up in love.

2. Make some notes on this passage. How was Paul describing the church in this passage? What is the significance of the metaphors that he used?

We all have a responsibility to help each other learn and grow. As we study the Bible and try to live in light of the truth we find there, we should naturally use the insight we gain to teach the other people in our lives. No matter how much knowledge you gain or how deeply you may be affected by the truth of the Bible, you will not be operating as a member of the body of Christ until you start investing in the lives of the Christians around you.

This may mean that you need to change the way you view the people around you. If you view them as unimportant, or if you tend to think of them as tools to help you get what you want, then you probably won't spend the time and effort to help them grow. But if you believe that you are both members of the same body, then you will do anything you can to help them.

3. Try to assess the way you view the other people in your life. Is there anything about the way you think about and view them that keeps you from investing in their lives?

4. How should the biblical pictures of the church as a body, a family, and a close-knit community change the way you think and push you to invest in the people around you?

Even if you get your personal Bible study on track and decide to invest in the people around you, you may still need to overcome obstacles. The reality of living in the twenty-first century is that we're all busier than we'd like to be, and many of us are busier than we ought to be. If you are going to reclaim the biblical model of speaking truth into the lives of the people around you, you will most likely need to rearrange your priorities, schedule, and daily routines. This means changing your lifestyle. If that sounds drastic, keep in mind that the Western church does not always do a good job of living out God's intention for His church. Recovering our role as the church may require you to restructure your life around the gospel.

5. Think through your schedule and daily routines. What aspects of your lifestyle are obstacles to spending the necessary time and energy to help the other Christians in your life learn and grow?

6. Take a minute to consider what steps you would need to take in order to overcome these obstacles. Make some notes below.

Paul's statement that we ought to speak the truth in love is simple yet profound. We all know people who are afraid to speak the truth, and people who speak the truth but not in love. So while we should all be teaching one another, we need to be careful about how we do it.

One of the best ways to learn how to teach is to learn from the example of the other people in your life—both good and bad. Most likely, you have experienced times when people have taught you in a way that was both informative and uplifting. Think through what it was that made those teaching times effective. You have probably also experienced times when people have taught you in a way that offended, confused, or degraded you. Even in these cases it can be helpful to think about those situations so you can pinpoint what you ought to avoid.

7. Think about the times when someone in your life took the time to teach you about something he or she had been learning. In the columns below, write down a few things that people have done well—things worth imitating—and a few things that people have done poorly—things worth avoiding.

Things that people have done well	Things that people have done poorly

Perhaps the biggest danger that comes when we start teaching other people is pride. There is something about the act of teaching that can make the teachers feel superior. If we're not careful, we will quickly become arrogant and condescending in the way we interact with the people around us. Pride is insidious, blinding, and relentless. Unless you work diligently to build humility into your character, any role you take on, even if it's for the sake of serving other people, will be tainted with pride.

One of the best ways to keep pride in check is to remember that you're teaching God's truth. None of us should be teaching people things that we have come up with on our own. Instead, we should be searching the Bible for God's truth and then sharing that truth with the people around us. If all we're doing is passing on the truth that God has given us, then what grounds do we have for pride? As Paul said, "Who sees anything different in you? What do you have that you did not receive? If then you received it, why do you boast as if you did not receive it?" (1 Corinthians 4:7).

8. Think through your personality, tendencies, and lifestyle. How can you begin shaping your thoughts and habits in order to stay humble?

In light of your calling to bless the people in your life, begin thinking through what God has been teaching you. This is where good intentions become reality. It's important to begin thinking of the people God has placed in your life while you study the Bible. How might you use what God has been teaching you to be a blessing to them?

9. Write down one or two things that God has been teaching you lately. Which people in your life right now might benefit from learning about what God is teaching you? How might you begin talking to them about these truths?

10. Before you end this session, spend some time in prayer. Ask God to give you a heart for the other people in your life. Ask Him to teach you from His Word and to guide you in how to best use those truths to invest in the lives of others. And be sure to ask God to keep you humble as you teach His truths to other people.

PRAYER
Session 1

Members of the early church devoted themselves to prayer. They had witnessed firsthand Jesus' life and ministry, and they understood what it meant to follow Him. Every time I begin reading the book of Acts, I'm struck by the enormity of what that small group of believers was supposed to accomplish. They were huddled together in a room, knowing that Jesus had sent them to be His witnesses throughout the known world and beyond, but not having a clue as to how to accomplish this task.

So what did they do? They prayed.

I'm convinced that we don't take prayer seriously because we don't understand the depth of our need for God to work supernaturally in our lives. Regardless of how confident we may feel, we are completely dependent on God for every breath we take and every action we perform. This means that if we are really going to live out our calling as the church, then we need to devote ourselves to prayer.

Use this session to examine your prayer life. Maybe you never take the time to stop and pray. Or maybe you're a committed prayer warrior. Either way, it's healthy to slow down and rethink your prayer life. How should we approach God in prayer? What is the purpose of prayer? What does it mean to be devoted to prayer? As you read through this session and answer the questions, push yourself to get back to the heart of prayer. This isn't about a technique or a routine; it's about coming humbly before God and begging Him to work in and around you.

Start by analyzing what you have done in the past. Try not to be defensive with this. Open yourself up and try to get to the heart of the way you tend to approach God in prayer.

1. Think back to any of your recent times of prayer. Based on these prayers, describe the way you tend to talk to God.

Ecclesiastes calls us to think about what we're doing when we approach God. Our culture tends to be very familiar, very casual, and we often have a hard time with showing respect for authority. But Ecclesiastes puts things in perspective: God is in heaven, and we are on earth, so we should address Him accordingly.

Read Ecclesiastes 5:1–7. Don't read too quickly, but allow yourself to soak it in and take it to heart. Once you've thought about the passage for a while, work through the questions below.

2. How does this passage describe God, mankind, and the way we should
   approach God? Don't rush through this. As you write your descriptions,
   allow yourself to feel the weight of what the passage is saying.

3. Ecclesiastes warns against being overly casual or apathetic when you
   approach God. Analyze your prayer life in light of this warning. How might
   you need to adjust the way you approach God in prayer?

4. Ecclesiastes also warns against flippantly making vows. It even says that
   it's better not to make a vow than to make a vow and not keep it. Clearly
   God wants us to be committed to the Christian life, so how do we balance
   this warning about vows with the need to let go of everything and follow
   Jesus?

As we consider these warnings about approaching God with the utmost respect, it's also important to keep in mind that we are called to approach God as a loving Father. We are even told to refer to Him as "Abba" (Romans 8:14–17), which is the most intimate Hebrew term for a father, comparable to saying "Daddy." This doesn't negate the warnings in Ecclesiastes, but it does give us a more complete picture of the way we are called to relate to God.

When we think of God as our Father, it doesn't mean that we immediately import all of the connotations that come from our own relationships with our earthly fathers. For many people, it's difficult to view God as a father because they have complicated or negative feelings about their fathers. But when the Bible describes God as our Father, it portrays Him as our loving provider who cares deeply about us. There is discipline involved (Hebrews 12:5–11), but it is the faithful correction of a loving Father who knows what is best for us.

Most of all, the imagery of God as our Father speaks of intimacy. This doesn't mean that we lose the respect for God that Ecclesiastes calls us to. We tend to think of these two concepts as mutually exclusive traits: Either we respect and fear God, or we love and trust Him. But this mentality is a fairly recent cultural development. At the same time that we respect, fear, and submit to God, we can also trust that He loves us deeply and wants us to maintain a close personal relationship with Him. This is what the biblical concept of a father is all about. Because of God's character, He is worthy of our love and respect simultaneously.

5. In light of the truth that God is our loving Father, how might you need to adjust the way you approach God in prayer?

6. How should these two paradoxical truths (God is our almighty Lord who demands complete respect; God is our loving Father who wants us to cry out to Him as our daddy) fit together in your prayer life? How should these truths be reflected in the way you address God, in the way you talk to Him, and in the things you ask Him?

Another important corrective for the way we pray is found in James 4. In speaking about the fights and quarrels that exist between believers, James pointed out that even our prayer lives are often characterized by the same type of self-centered struggles.

Read James 4:1–4. As you read, try to get a handle on the implications of this passage for your prayer life. When you've finished reading, work through the questions below.

7. James was clear that we often don't get what we need because we don't pray. How has prayerlessness affected your relationship with God? How might your Christian life change if you simply began asking God to work in your life?

8. James also pointed out that our prayers often go unanswered because we are asking with the wrong motives. Can you think of times when you've asked God for things with the wrong motives? What can you do to ensure that the motives behind your prayers are right?

It's important that we really think about what we're praying, rather than just repeating phrases mindlessly. Everyone prays a little bit differently, but most people end their prayers by saying, "In Jesus' name, amen." Jesus taught us to pray in His name (John 14:13), but what is the significance of this?

When we pray in Jesus' name, we are claiming solidarity with Jesus. We are identifying ourselves with Him and acknowledging that His mission is also our mission. We are saying that the things we are asking are the same things that Jesus would be asking for. So if all our prayers are focused on our own desires and not on Jesus' kingdom and mission in this world, then it doesn't make any sense for us to claim that we are praying in Jesus' name.

9. How would you need to adjust your lifestyle, motivations, and thought processes in order to truly begin praying in Jesus' name?

10. If you were going to truly pray in Jesus' name right now, what things would Jesus have you pray for? Make a list below.

As you close this session, don't simply move on. Try to take everything you've thought through in this session and apply it to your prayer life. Do everything you can to make prayer an indispensable part of your life and to approach prayer in light of the notes you made in this session. Prayer shouldn't be an add-on to your busy life. It should be the driving force that empowers everything you do as you seek to follow Jesus in the power of the Holy Spirit.

11. Finally, spend time praying about the items you listed under question 10. Pause before you pray to make sure that you're approaching God appropriately. See Him as the almighty God who is in heaven and the loving Father who is always near to you.

PRAYER
Session 2

As we mentioned in the previous session, prayer was an integral part of the early church. It wasn't something that they had to make into a program; it was a natural response to the intense setting in which they lived and the impossible task that they had been given.

I believe that it's both possible and essential for us to begin treating prayer in the same way. Our mission is the same as theirs, and God wants us to integrate prayer so deeply into our being that we can't imagine what life would be like without it.

In the previous session, you analyzed the content of your prayer life and your approach to God in light of some key warnings in Ecclesiastes and James. This session will focus on taking steps to develop a committed and consistent prayer life. Use this session to build prayer into your lifestyle for the purpose of accomplishing your God-given mission.

Start by analyzing the frequency and intensity of your prayer life. Most of us have a tendency to make our prayer lives sound better than they really are. As you begin this session, be as honest with yourself as possible. It's not about where you've gone wrong; it's about getting yourself on track for the future. If the church is going to function in the way that God designed it, we will all need to place a high priority on actively depending on God through prayer.

1. Up to this point, how would you describe your prayer life?

In most cases, the amount of time a person spends in prayer reflects his or her view of God. A person who is constantly asking God to act in her life is exemplifying her belief that she desperately needs God in everything. On the other hand, a person who never stops to pray is exemplifying her belief that God is irrelevant to her daily life. This is an oversimplification, but we cannot deny the fact that our true beliefs manifest themselves in our actions. Regardless of what we say we believe, our actions reveal our fundamental assumptions about life.

2. Do you think the amount of time you spend in prayer reflects your view of God? How so?

Making prayer an integral part of your life will require you to stay focused on why you're praying. The early church prayed because they had been commissioned by Jesus to do the impossible. Prayer flowed naturally from their dedication to their mission and the urgency they felt.

But what about us? What is the mission that we are trying to accomplish? Well, it's as simple and as profound as following Jesus. As we seek to follow Him in our daily lives—doing the things that He did and obeying the things that He commanded us to do—we are fulfilling our God-given mission. Though it will look a little different in our modern setting, the mission is the same for us as it was for the early church.

Jesus called His followers to go into all the world and make disciples. This means teaching others to obey everything that He commanded and baptizing them. And it remains the mission of the church to this day. Christianity is not about each of us individually going to heaven when we die; it's about continuing Jesus' mission to seek and to save the lost. It's about helping other people to see who Jesus is and to see His love, joy, and peace reign in their lives. We join together in fellowship, teach one another, pray, and share in communion so that we can work together to accomplish this mission.

If you keep this mission in mind, and if you stay focused on fearing God, following Jesus, and relying on the Holy Spirit, then prayer should become a natural and essential part of your life. You will clearly see the needs around you and instinctively ask God to work in your situation.

3. Take a minute to think through what this mission should look like in your unique setting. If you are going to accomplish this mission, what will have to happen? Don't settle for easy answers here. Make some clear notes about what attitudes would need to change, which people would need

to be supernaturally influenced, and what barriers would have to come down.

As you think about reshaping your prayer life, it's important to keep in mind the fellowship we discussed earlier. You're not on this mission alone, so as you think through what to pray about, don't forget about the other Christians in your life. Part of the fellowship that you share should involve praying for one another.

4. As you think about the other Christians in your life, what do they need to learn or do in order to be a part of accomplishing God's mission in your setting? What help or encouragement do they need from God? Being as specific as possible, make some notes about how you can be praying for each of them.

5. Using the things you noted under questions 3 and 4 as a starting point, break this list into specific prayer requests. Beginning today, commit yourself to praying for each of these things on a regular basis.

Now that you've considered what God would want you to be doing in the specific setting in which He has placed you, it's worth thinking through the essential role of prayer in fulfilling this mission.

6. For the sake of illustrating the importance of prayer, spend a few minutes considering two different scenarios. In the first scenario, describe what your mission might look like if you completely neglected prayer for the rest of your life. What might your mission look like if you dedicated all of your skill and effort but never prayed? In the second scenario, describe what your mission might look like if you absolutely devoted yourself to prayer from this moment on. Make some notes below.

Without Prayer

With Prayer

One of Jesus' most intriguing stories is the parable of the persistent widow. In the parable, Jesus described a woman who needed to receive justice in some matter. Unfortunately, the judge was unjust and would not listen to her case. Yet the widow eventually received justice because she persistently came back again and again until the judge heard her cause.

Read Luke 18:1–8. As you read the parable, consider what Jesus is trying to teach us about prayer. After reading the parable, answer the questions below.

7. Why do you think Jesus wants us to be so persistent in our prayers? Why wouldn't He simply give us what we ask for right when we ask for it?

8. What is the difference between the meaningless, repetitious prayers that Jesus condemned in Matthew 6 and the persistent prayers that He commended in Luke 18?

9. If you are a person who tends to be inconsistent in your prayer life, what would it take to discipline yourself to become persistent in asking God to help you accomplish the mission He has entrusted to you?

For many people, it takes more than desire to develop a strong prayer life. Most likely, in order to pray persistently you will need to free up some time in your schedule. Because we tend to place a strong emphasis on productivity, this may seem backward. You might feel like you need to be going out and "doing something." But don't assume that prayer is nothing. By praying persistently you are laboring to see God's kingdom come and His will done on earth, even as it is done in heaven. I can't urge you strongly enough to build consistent prayer times into your schedule.

In addition to regularly scheduled prayer times, the Bible calls us to "pray without ceasing" (1 Thessalonians 5:17). This can be a difficult thing to wrap our minds around, but it highlights the importance of prayer. This is not something we add on to our already busy lives; this is something we should be doing every minute of every day. This doesn't mean that you should stay home on your knees all day every day. But it might involve turning off the iPod and TV at specific times to allow yourself to think about and pray for God's kingdom to come. It may mean processing everything you encounter in the presence of God, asking Him what He thinks and how you should respond. It will probably look a little different for each person, depending on your unique situation. But the point is, God wants prayer to be a constant and essential part of your life.

10. Think through your daily routine. What might praying without ceasing look like in your specific situation?

As you close this session, do everything you can to keep from simply walking away without absolutely devoting yourself to prayer. If you are going to seriously pursue your calling to live out God's intention for His church, you will need to persistently pursue Him in prayer. This will require sacrifice, but as you experience more intimacy with God and see Him working in and around you, you won't regret a single minute that you devote to prayer.

11. End this session by praying. Try not to revert to any old prayer habits that you may have formed over the years. Instead, earnestly ask God to work in your situation. Ask Him to empower you to fulfill the mission He has called you to. And don't forget to pray for the other Christians God has placed in your life.

COMMUNION
Session 1

"Do this in remembrance of me." Jesus introduced Communion to His disciples with these words (Luke 22:19). It really is an important statement. It tells us that Jesus knew His followers would be prone to forget Him. Life constantly pulls us to think about other things, but Jesus established a ritual to call us back to what really matters. Every time we take Communion, we are given a fresh reminder of our Savior and what He did to set us free.

Jesus' words also tell us that He is worth remembering. I'm sure that sounds obvious, but how often do you find yourself thinking about Jesus—His life, His death, or His resurrection? No matter where we find ourselves in life, it's always important for us to remember Jesus. There is no activity, career, or stage of life in which remembering Jesus is not essential.

Unfortunately, we often forget what we're supposed to remember. I'm not suggesting that you'll wake up one day and realize that you've forgotten the content of the gospel. The truth is much subtler and more dangerous than that. I'm suggesting that you could very easily get so caught up in your career, so enamored with the American Dream, so focused on church activities, so distracted by the busyness of life that one day you stop to think about your life and realize that you haven't been following Jesus. This type of forgetfulness is much more common and much more powerful. It's possible to talk a lot about Jesus while at the same time excluding Him from nearly every aspect of your life. Because Jesus established Communion as a means of remembering Him, it provides us with a perfect opportunity to pause and examine our lives.

1. As you ponder your thoughts and actions, to what extent would you say that you have forgotten about Jesus and the mission He has given you? Why do you say that?

Though Paul had certainly taught the Corinthian church the importance of Communion, he had to confront them because they were following the ritual of Communion but missing the point. Read 1 Corinthians 11:27–29. As you read, notice who Paul was confronting and what they were doing wrong. When you've finished meditating on the passage for a while, answer the questions below.

2. What was Paul warning against in this passage? What do you think he meant by eating and drinking "in an unworthy manner"? What did he mean by "discerning the body [of the Lord]"?

3. Think practically about your own experience with Communion. Do you think you have ever made any of the mistakes that the Corinthians made? What about other mistakes regarding Communion?

4. Paul warned against taking Communion in an unworthy manner. Try examining this passage the other way around. What would it mean to eat the bread and drink the cup of the Lord in a *worthy* manner?

In the verse immediately preceding this passage, Paul said that every time we take Communion, we "proclaim the Lord's death until he comes" (1 Corinthians 11:26). This is a significant statement, because we have a tendency to think that we only proclaim Jesus' death when we use words to preach the gospel. Paul suggested that the symbolism inherent in the act of Communion is a proclamation of the gospel as well.

As you think through the power of Communion to proclaim Christ, consider how much more powerful this ritual becomes when it is backed by a lifestyle that proclaims those same truths. When our lives demonstrate to the people around us that Jesus died to redeem us from our sins, rose again in victory over death, and supernaturally transforms and empowers us to follow Him, then the world hears a message far more powerful than a gospel tract.

5. Think through your daily routines. What would it mean for your actions to proclaim Jesus? What type of things can you do and say that would point people to the truths of the gospel?

6. Can you point to any aspects of your life that proclaim Jesus? How so? If not, why do you think this is?

Communion is a powerful reminder of the mission we have been called to. As we've already considered, so many things in our lives distract us from our calling to follow Jesus. We need reminders to call us back to what really matters.

We all have the capacity to remind the Christians in our lives of their calling to follow Jesus. But we also have the capacity to add to the distractions and pull people further away from their mission. An important part of living out the truths that Communion symbolizes is to help remind our fellow Christians of their calling to follow Jesus.

7. Do you tend to push the other Christians around you toward following Jesus, or do you tend to pull them away from this? How so?

Many Christians find themselves caught off guard when an opportunity to take Communion arrives. I can recall many times when the bread and the cup have been an abrupt reminder of what I had forgotten. Of course, this is why Jesus built the reminder of Communion into the life of the church. But imagine if Communion didn't catch you by surprise. Imagine greeting the bread and the cup with a smile because they symbolize the very truths your life has been devoted to. This is something we should all work toward: a lifestyle that is consistent with the truths we claim to hold dear.

8. What steps—big or small—can you take right now to prepare yourself for Communion? How can you adjust your lifestyle so that Communion becomes a natural outflow of your life?

9. Before ending this session, spend some time in prayer. We have been talking about some weighty truths, and it would be easy to let them slip by without truly appreciating their significance. Take some time to thank God for the gift we've been given in the life, death, and resurrection of Jesus Christ. Ask Him to empower you through the Spirit to live a life that truly proclaims these incredible truths.

A Note on Doing Communion in Your Small Group

In your first discussion of the film *COMMUNION*, we challenged you to take Communion as a small group rather than during a traditional church service. I'd like to take a minute to help you think through how this might play out in your specific context. First, I want to point out some potentially sensitive issues related to Communion. Then I'd like to help guide you through a simple but meaningful approach to taking Communion as a group.

Communion is all about unity, but ironically, it has often become a divisive issue in the church. Depending on your group dynamics, your denominational affiliations, and the traditions you're accustomed to, you may need to be very sensitive about changing the way your church approaches Communion. In some denominations, for example, Communion must be presided over by a licensed or ordained minister. If this is the case, invite that person to join your group for an evening so he or she can lead you in taking Communion, or ask that person to help you think through the challenges in the *COMMUNION* film in light of your specific context.

You may also want to invite other members of your church to join you in taking Communion. This could be a good opportunity to help refocus a larger portion of your church body on your God-given mission.

There are many different ways to approach Communion. Many people choose to incorporate Communion into a shared meal. If you want to use this approach, you can gather your group together for a meal and pause to take Communion before, during, or after the meal. The fellowship that comes through sharing a meal can make your Communion time more meaningful, but it's not essential.

When you're ready to take Communion together, I recommend keeping the ritual simple, but make sure it retains its significance. Evangelicals tend to shy away from rituals, but sometimes we risk underplaying the significance of the thing we are trying to commemorate. Rituals are only bad when we lose sight of the truths they are meant to convey.

When Jesus instituted the Lord's Supper, He took the bread from the table and used it to commemorate His body, which would be broken for His people. In the same way, He took a cup of wine and used it to commemorate His blood (Matthew 26:26–29). When you gather to take Communion as a group, you will need some type of bread and some type of wine (though some Christians choose to use grape juice because of personal convictions about alcohol).

When you're ready to take Communion, you could have someone read 1 Corinthians 11:23–25 (or through to verse 29). Consider asking someone to remind the group of your mission together and how remembering Jesus' life and sacrifice helps you to stay focused on that mission. Then take Communion together. Close your Communion time in prayer, asking God to empower your group to live in light of who Jesus is and what He has done.

Again, don't worry about doing Communion "just right." Jesus called us to take Communion as a reminder, so the important thing is that you take time to remember. Also keep in mind that while taking Communion in this type of setting may feel new and exciting now, it could easily become a mindless ritual over time. Make sure that you are constantly calling each other to remember and put into practice the truths that Communion symbolizes.

COMMUNION
Session 2

Over the past several weeks, we've examined a number of areas in which the church seems to have lost sight of its mission. As important and essential as the church is, it's healthy for us to realize that our church gatherings are not perfect and we are certainly not infallible. The church is supernatural in the sense that it is made up of a group of believers who are empowered by the Holy Spirit to fulfill God's purposes on earth. But since we are all human beings and therefore prone to distraction and forgetfulness, our churches are in constant need of reformation. As soon as we get comfortable with the way we do church, we're probably missing something important.

A healthy church does not mean a perfect church. Rather, a healthy church is made up of a group of believers with a commitment to the church and a desire to keep bringing it back in line with God's purposes. For many people, the church's imperfections are enough to make them walk away from the corruptions of organized religion. But if we want to fulfill God's purposes on earth, we simply cannot give up on the church.

We could probably think of a number of approaches that God could have chosen for spreading His kingdom on earth, but when Jesus ascended to heaven, He left the church to finish His task. Jesus said that He would build His church, and the gates of hell would not prevail against it (Matthew 16:18). Being committed to God's mission for us means being committed to His church—for better or worse, in good times and bad.

1. Would you say that you're absolutely committed to maintaining and expanding God's church? Why do you say this?

The author of Hebrews gave us some important insight into what Jesus accomplished and how we should function with regard to the other Christians in our lives. Take some time to carefully and thoughtfully read Hebrews 10:19–25. Reflect on what the passage calls us to do as well as the theological basis the passage gives for doing these things.

2. According to verses 19–23, what should the work of Jesus lead you to do? Don't give this a quick answer; try to flesh it out a bit.

3. According to verses 24–25, what is your responsibility to the other Christians in your life? Don't give an abstract answer here. Write out your answer with regard to the specific people God has placed in your life.

Rather than simply waiting for our churches to become what we feel they ought to be, we all have to take seriously this calling to "stir up" the other Christians in our lives. I've already mentioned that the problems in our churches cause some people to give up on church and pursue their own individualistic take on the Christian life. There are also a number of people who have not left their churches but who have given up on trying to help their churches change. Many of these people have made attempts to "fix" their churches but met with so much opposition, frustration, and failure that they have simply resigned themselves to church as it is, rather than church as it ought to be.

4. Have you ever made any attempts to fix the church? If so, what lessons have you learned from what you've done well and what you've done poorly? If not, why do you think you've never tried to get involved with this?

Sometimes our attempts to reform the church meet with failure because we try to put the cart before the horse. We pursue fellowship, teaching, prayer, communion, and a number of other things as though they are ends in themselves. But as good as these things are, they are means of accomplishing what God has placed us on this earth to accomplish.

We may be able to get a group of people excited about fellowship for a while, but if that fellowship does not have a greater purpose, then sooner or later their interest will fade. If we remember that fellowship helps us to spur one another on to following Jesus, making disciples, and seeing God's will done here on earth, however, then our fellowship will be lively and inspiring rather than forced.

5. How can you focus your fellowship, teaching, prayer, and communion on the goal of accomplishing your mission rather than pursuing these things as ends in themselves?

As much as you may be committed to seeing your church change for the better, ambiguity often leads to inaction. Pinpointing some problem areas in the church can help you identify a good starting point.

6. Make a list of the problems you see with the church in general. Try not to be overly critical with this. Just be earnest: How does the church need to change in order to recapture its God-given purpose?

You may not be able to change the entire church around the world, but you can begin making strides toward reforming your own group of Christians and your church. As you assess your church, make sure that your motivation is to see the bride of Christ become more pure and effective in accomplishing its mission.

7. Give this some serious thought: What steps can you take—whether big or small—to steer your gathering of Christians or your church toward its God-given purpose?

Changing *anything* about your church may sound like a daunting task. This is especially true when you start rethinking key aspects of your church's life. Without a doubt, you will encounter many people who want things to stay the way they've always been. In some respects it would probably be easier for you to try to recover God's intention for His church on your own. You may even be able to find a few likeminded people who are willing to work with you. Even if you're committed to your church, and even if you've decided not to leave and do your own thing, you're going to find people who are simply not on board with what you're doing. The easiest option will be to leave these people behind.

But as soon as you give up on the people around you, you've given up on God's plan for His church. If you boldly lead the charge with a few like-minded people while neglecting those who have a hard time with the changes you want to make, you will be making steady strides toward a church split. I don't know of a special way to preserve unity in a situation like this, but I know that unity is worth fighting for, and patience is key. Any change worth fighting for is also worth waiting for; not everything has to change overnight. As you think through the things you can do to help your church change for the better, make sure you think through the best way to lovingly and patiently work with the people who will be resistant to the changes you're trying to make.

8. How can you work toward change in some key areas of your church's life while at the same time patiently helping resistant church members get on board?

9. As you end this session, spend some time in prayer. The task you are pursuing is not easy. The fight will be difficult, and it will last your entire lifetime—no church is beyond the need for constant reformation. Ask God to give you the strength, patience, and guidance to play your part in making the church what He desires it to be.

BASIC.LIVING
Final Session

Most often, the basic truths are the most important. There are some difficult truths in the Bible (2 Peter 3:16), but the essence of Christianity is fairly simple. Jesus calls us to pursue a childlike faith (Mark 10:14–15) and pushes us to very simply do what He says (Luke 6:46).

Many people are intimidated by Christianity, thinking that it necessarily involves mastering a complicated theology and adhering to a rigid list of moral standards. The Bible does call us to use our minds and pursue the knowledge of God, and we are called to imitate Jesus and pursue perfection. But these things are not as complicated as we often make them.

Jesus took all of the Old Testament Law and summarized it under two points: "You shall love the Lord your God with all your heart and with all your soul and with all your mind. This is the great and first commandment. And a second is like it: You shall love your neighbor as yourself. On these two commandments depend all the Law and the Prophets"

(Matthew 22:37–40). It all comes down to those two things—love God, love people.

For whatever reason, however, we have a tendency to see complex truths and deeper meanings as more important than simple, basic truths. I see this as backward. I'm not saying there isn't a place for profound truths in the Christian life. But I do want to suggest that we should be keeping our eyes open for the obvious truths. The deeper truths will come in time, but we won't recognize them if we miss the obvious truths. When we approach God's Word, then, we should take every word at face value and consider how our lives would change if we began to live out the simple truths of the Bible.

1. When you sit down to read your Bible, would you say that you focus on the basic truths, or do you look for profound, esoteric truths? If you focus on the latter, why do you think you have this tendency?

Focusing on basic truths is one thing, but it gets much more difficult when we begin to apply them to our lives. Application is the whole point. We want to read God's Word, understand His truth, and be changed by it. This process needs to be a fundamental part of our lives as Christians. It can be difficult to build this process into your life, especially if you've developed other habits, but it is absolutely worth working toward.

2. Have you been able to develop a pattern of pulling basic truths from the Bible and applying them to your life? If so, briefly describe your pattern. If not, what do you think has kept you from getting to this point?

One of the biggest obstacles to taking the Scriptures at face value is the reality that we all carry our baggage with us into our Bible studies. We all have cognitive assumptions about life, God, the human condition, the Bible, and many other things. We also carry baggage with regard to who or what we fear, trust, desire, love, hate, etc. These deep-seated emotional connections can be incredibly powerful, yet we rarely consider how they affect us. When we read the Bible (when we look at anything in the world, in fact), all of these assumptions come together to form a lens through which we interpret and respond to what we're reading.

This set of assumptions can also be described as a worldview. Everyone has a worldview, whether they are aware of it or not. The point is not to get rid of your worldview (this is impossible) but to identify what your fundamental assumptions are so that you can assess them in light of God's truth. For example, many people assume that there are no supernatural forces or events in this world. This fundamental assumption is known as naturalism. A person holding this assumption will read biblical passages about Jesus healing the sick, walking on water, and raising the dead and conclude that these things can't be literally true: They must either be lies or spiritual metaphors.

This person will also have difficulty with the biblical teaching on the Holy Spirit. The point is, our assumptions can have a big impact on whether or not we're open to taking the Bible at face value.

Ideally, every time we expose ourselves to the Bible, our thinking and emotions come more in line with God's truth. Then when we approach the Bible again, our worldview is more biblical and we are more open to clearly seeing what God wants to tell us. As this cycle continues, we become increasingly less conformed to this world and increasingly more transformed by the renewing of our minds. So as you seek to develop a lifestyle of looking for and living out the basic truths of Scripture, try to examine your assumptions so that you can evaluate them according to the truth of the Bible.

3. What assumptions do you think you bring to the Scriptures when you read them? How might these assumptions lead you to wrong conclusions about what the Bible is saying?

Letting go of our assumptions and taking the Bible at face value is a lifelong process. Our fundamental assumptions about life and the way the world works are always deeply rooted, and it can be very difficult to evaluate these in light of God's truth. But the difficulty does not stop with reading the Bible.

Many people know exactly what God is calling them to do, but they have become content to know and not do. In your group discussion, you talked about James' warning against hearing the Word of God and not doing what it says. Once you begin reading the Bible to find the basic truths that God is calling you to, you will be faced with an important decision: How will you respond?

Whenever we decide to live in simple obedience to the basic commands of Scripture, we will be faced with opposition. As easy as obedience sounds and as simple as the process may be, serious obstacles are inevitable. Sometimes we will be fighting against ourselves as we try to rationalize our behavior or convince ourselves that the Bible isn't really saying what it seems to be saying. At other times we will be drawn away or distracted by the people, possessions, and activities in our lives. Sometimes it will be our own selfish desires that pull us away from following Jesus. The point is, this won't be an easy process. In fact, following Jesus will be a lifelong battle. But it's a battle worth fighting, and you can prepare yourself by trying to identify the obstacles you will face. The next two questions present two different types of simple commands. Read the commands and think through the obstacles involved in each case. How can you overcome these obstacles and obediently follow these commands?

4. Paul said, "Do not be anxious about anything" (Philippians 4:6). What obstacles do you face in obeying this command? How can you begin making progress toward simple obedience in this area?

5. Jesus said, "Give to the one who begs from you, and do not refuse the one who would borrow from you" (Matthew 5:42). What obstacles do you face in obeying this command? How can you begin making progress toward simple obedience in this area?

Before closing this study, take some time to think about how your life has been affected. No doubt you have been challenged by a number of things over the past several weeks. Think over what you've learned from the four films you watched (*FELLOWSHIP, TEACHING, PRAYER,* and *COMMUNION*), your group discussions, and your own personal study. Don't allow yourself to go back to life as usual. Think about these truths and how they should continue to affect your thinking and lifestyle.

6. As you think back over the truths that have challenged you over the past several weeks, which things stand out as especially important? List a few things below.

7. For each of the items you listed above, write out a few action points. What specific actions can you begin taking right now to address these issues?

I would hate for you to leave this study and think that it's all about actions. There are many things that we've been called to do, but central to all of these actions is our relationship with God. If we're not fearing God, following Jesus, and relying on the Holy Spirit, then all of our actions will be frustrating, vain, and fruitless. Take some time to consider the health of your relationship with God.

8. How has your relationship with God changed as a result of the things you've been studying?

9. How does your relationship with God still need to change? How can you begin working toward this end?

My prayer is that you won't see this as an end but as a beginning, or even just an encouragement on your journey. BASIC is all about seeing who God is and responding appropriately. It's about identifying God's mission for your life and devoting yourself to that mission, using the resources He has given you and loving the people He has placed in your life. Take these basic concepts and enjoy the fellowship with God and other Christians that comes as we work together to accomplish God's purposes on this earth.

10. Spend some time in prayer. Ask God to cement these truths in your life. Ask Him to empower you through the Holy Spirit to labor with supernatural wisdom and power as you seek to fulfill your mission on earth. Ask God for the honesty to approach His Word humbly, to take His basic truths at face value, and to live them out in your life.

Tips for Leaders

A good discussion leader doesn't need to have all the answers. Only God has all the answers about being the church, and as the leader, you will probably end up learning more about being the church than anyone in your group.

Discussion Leader's Job Description

Your job is simply to:

- Prepare for each meeting

- Keep the discussion moving so that it doesn't get stuck on one question

- Make sure everyone has a chance to talk and no one dominates (it is not necessary that every person respond aloud to every question, but every person should have a chance to do so)

- Bring the discussion back on track if it veers off on a tangent

- Decide when to move on to the next question

- Make sure the discussion remains respectful

Preparing for the Discussion

The discussion questions are on the DVD discs for the four films under the "Session 1" and "Session 2" headings respectively. All of the discussion questions appear on-screen. As you cycle through the questions, video clips from the film will pop up to provide context and reminders. As you come to each question, have someone read it aloud. Likewise, you can have someone read the Bible passage aloud when you get to it.

It's a good idea to review the questions before each meeting. If you can, view the film as well.

It may be helpful to arrange chairs in a U shape around the television so that everyone can see the screen and one another. You'll want to dim the lights in the room somewhat so that the screen is clear, but provide enough light so that people can see one another's faces. (You could darken the room to view the film and then turn on a light for your discussion.)

Also, pray before each meeting for the Spirit's leading. Ask Him to help you sense His guidance as you lead the discussion. I have not provided you with right answers to the questions. In some cases the right answer is whatever the Spirit is saying to your unique group. In other cases some answers are more true to the Bible than others, and if you're not sure your group is on track, you can ask your pastor, do some research on your own, or investigate books on the subject.

Most important of all, spend time praying for your group. You can't talk anyone into being in true fellowship with others. Pray that the Spirit of God would fill your lives and do the impossible in and through you. In the book of Acts, the human actors were just ordinary, weak people, but the Holy Spirit accomplished unbelievable things through these ordinary people as they prayed and submitted themselves to following His leading. May that be the case with your group.

Guiding the Discussion

A few ground rules can make the discussion deeper:

- *Confidentiality:* Whatever is said in the group stays in the group. Nothing is to be repeated to those who weren't there.

- *Honesty:* We're not here to impress each other. We're here to grow and to know each other.

- *Respect:* Disagreement is welcome. Disrespect is not.

The discussion should be a conversation among the group members, not a one-on-one with the leader. You can encourage this with statements like "Thanks, Allison. What does everyone else think?" or "Does anyone have a similar experience, or a different one?"

Don't be afraid of silence—it means group members are thinking about how to answer a question. Trust the Spirit, and wait. Sometimes it's helpful to rephrase the question in your own words. Then wait for others' responses, and avoid jumping in with your own.

I encourage you to be honest with the members of your group. If you desire to grow and change, you will motivate others to do the same. Be open about areas in which you welcome the group's prayer and support. Allow people to challenge your thinking.

Answers that are true to biblical teaching are important, but I am most concerned that people may study God and never *know* Him, never be *changed* by Him. I am afraid that people will learn what the church is supposed to be and do but never act on that knowledge. With every session, keep asking yourself and your group: "How should this change us? If we really committed ourselves to being the church and doing the Father's will, what would He have us do? Where would He have us go?" At the end of the day, it's about following Jesus in the power of the Spirit in order to accomplish what God has placed us on this earth to do. It's about advancing the kingdom of God. It's about His will being done on earth as in heaven.

WE ARE CHURCH

BASIC SERIES
featuring FRANCIS CHAN

BASIC is a seven-part series of short films that challenges us to be the church as described in Scripture.

What is church? You are church. I am church. *We are church.*

FEAR GOD
FOLLOW JESUS
HOLY SPIRIT
FELLOWSHIP
TEACHING
PRAYER
COMMUNION

BASICSERIES.COM

FLANNEL
.org

David©Cook
transforming lives together